I Have a Dream

Inaugural Poems for a New Generation

I Have a Dream

Inaugural Poems for a New Generation

By San Mateo County Youth

A Special Project by the San Mateo County Arts Commission
Edited by Aileen Cassinetto & Jim Ward
Foreword by Robin Rodricks
San Mateo County, California, 2021

Book Design by C. Sophia Ibardaloza
Printed and Bound in The United States of America

Library of Congress Control Number: 2020925908

SAN MATEO COUNTY BOARD OF SUPERVISORS
https://bos.smcgov.org

SAN MATEO COUNTY ARTS COMMISSION
https://cmo.smcgov.org/arts-commission

SAN MATEO COUNTY POET LAUREATE
www.sanmateocountypoet.org | www.aileencassinetto.com

To a more equitable and more perfect union.

TABLE OF CONTENTS

FOREWORD

Poetry — and the arts — help both the writer and the audience process and give voice to thoughts and feelings, which very often lead to social action. The youth of today are living through a pandemic, and civil unrest from institutional racism. How they respond to these circumstances will determine their future and the future of society as a whole. Their voices and actions, reflecting visions and dreams for a better tomorrow, will help us all as we struggle with the present, and work towards achieving a more just society.

The Arts Commission is committed to a healthy and vibrant community, and to connecting and inspiring every aspect of the diverse lives in San Mateo County. Nothing gives me more hope for a better society than that of voices of our youth speaking out — not just for themselves, but for all of us. And I truly believe in what author Johann Goedte wrote, that "At the moment of commitment, the world conspires to assist you." Thank you, Poets, for putting your visions and dreams to paper and agreeing to having them published here — in doing so you have taken the first step in your commitment to contributing to a better world.

Robin Rodricks
Director Emerita of the San Mateo County Arts Commission

PREFACE

At this inflection point in our nation's history, finding writing opportunities that are purposeful, impactful and timely is challenging. When the inaugural poem contest was presented to my students, I felt it would be a wonderful opportunity for them to share their voice and vision regarding their place in our country. Students were encouraged to look back at their past, at their present as teenagers in today's society, and their consideration of the future. Students at this age are in constant movement and full of incredible energy coming from many places. Their unique voices need to be heard and considered. As Walt Whitman said, "I am large. I contain multitudes." This is certainly true of not only teenagers, but all of us as Americans.

Poetry can be an elusive topic to teach. First and foremost, I hope students recognize it as a "snapshot" of a moment or place in time. I want them to feel it as alive and beautiful, as well as provocative and unnerving. I wish for them to recognize the power present in the eloquence and flow of words coming from their voices and their hearts of who they are at this point in their sojourn, and moving forward in their lives. That is, to me, the joy of teaching these wonderful students- to get to walk with them and know them, for a little while, on this part of the pathway they travel.

As with all positive writing projects, this has been a collaborative journey. Many deep and heartfelt thanks to Poet Laureate Aileen Cassinetto for earnestly working with these students on their writing and sharing with them the life of a poet. Also, thanks to Julie Smith at the Half Moon Bay Public Library for bringing opportunities for the celebration of the written word to our coastal community. And finally, thanks to the students here for opening their hearts and minds to sharing the words we have here.

With respect and gratitude,

Jim Ward
Teacher (English, AVID IV & ELD)
Fall Play & Spring Musical Director
Half Moon Bay High School

INTRODUCTION

We begin with hope. This is perhaps why poems were traditional New Year's gifts—for what is poetry but a stockpile of possibilities. The past year has been shaped by the coronavirus pandemic, by economic recession and racial unrest, by distance learning and social distancing, and what was possibly the most gripping election in US history. But it was also defined by the generosity of our neighbors and the kindness of strangers.

The idea for this anthology came about after more than 100 of our county's high school students spent the last month of 2020 attending poetry workshops and crafting inaugural poems. Partly inspired by the Academy of American Poets' 2021 Inaugural Poem Contest, we challenged San Mateo County's youth to write about their views, their experiences and their hopes for America. Our purpose is not only to amplify the voices of our young people, but also acknowledge that they are co-authors of our national and community narrative, and of the spaces which they inhabit.

San Mateo County in Northern California is home to over 158,000 youth under the age of 18, who were raised in the age of technology: as an example, 90 of this anthology's contributors are Gen Zers born the same year as Facebook; the others, ages 10 and below, belong to Generation Alpha, born around the time (or after) "app" was voted word of the year. As our youth explore and engage with digital innovations, it is our hope that they also gain a deeper appreciation for the nuances of language, to give voice to all that is possible and remarkable.

"We encounter each other in words…," writes Elizabeth Alexander, whose inaugural poem inspired many pieces in this collection. In crafting the poems in this anthology, our young people are embedding this particular moment in history with their identities and unique experiences, staking a claim to a future that is wholly theirs. And what a vision it is, to "come together / And... show [the world] what we can become."

Aileen Cassinetto
Poet Laureate of the County of San Mateo, California

AFTER JOSEPH R. BIDEN, JOHN F. KENNEDY, ABRAHAM LINCOLN, BARACK OBAMA & MARTIN LUTHER KING, JR.

Time to Heal in America: A Found Poem

United, there is little we cannot do: we are Americans, friends.
We are greater than the differences of faction.
Your kitchen table is like mine. You sit there at night.
And when the time comes
to reaffirm our enduring spirit, we can laugh
in the face of our common dangers.
Someone said we live among 300 billion stars.
Someone also said in space, we cannot cry
because there is no gravity to pull down
our tears. As the planets spin, so do our days.
But on earth, gravity holds up as much as it pulls down.
With the fierce urgency of now, we can build tomorrow
on the bedrock of science, mindful of the sacrifices
of our ancestors. What comes next is a choice we make—
look ahead, dare to dream, bind up America's wounds.
We are a nation of 300 million possibilities.
Count on me to bear the burden of a long twilight struggle.
At my kitchen table sit the doers and makers of things,
picking themselves up then marching ahead
as far as their dreams will take them.
Besides this, I have a dream today, that I, too, am
free at last, in this winter of hardship, unafraid and unashamed
to believe in the possibility of this country.
We are Americans, and the sky is full of stars, my friends.

DENELY ACOSTA

The Fear We Have

We fear our voices
We fear what comes next
We fear our health
We fear our lives to protect what we love

Today, tomorrow, later
The words gather the back of our mind like clocks ticking
We want the old times, we want new times
We want hanging with friends back we want future plans
There's been enough time. Enough fear.
Enough Tomorrows.
Enough Laters.

The long days, the cold evening, the fast dark nights
Is going nowhere.
Hoping for better days
Hoping for a miracle
Families hoping, children hoping, countries hoping
We as one we all together
Will find a way.

A way to cope
A way to feel

A way to find a solution
A way to thank god for those hard workers
A way to live again

EVAN ALEXANDER

Untitled

When nothing seems to be going in the right direction,
Hope is there to guide us through the mysterious forest of life.
When the cold hands of sadness grip our body, hope is always there
    pushing back.
When nothing good seems to be happening, hope is always there
    pushing us forward.

Hope is always there, helping somebody out.
A boy hopes for a new toy.
A businessman hopes for a better opportunity.
A teacher hopes their students will succeed.
A man hopes he can buy food tonight.

No matter how big or small, hope is always there.
It is the one thing that nobody can take away from us.
No matter how much pain or misery someone goes through,
    the ember of hope still remains.

Through hardship and adversity,
through challenges and sadness,
we push through as we have before into better times.
It is not always easy, but through strength and perseverance, we prevail.

We as people create our own future. We create success out of hardship.
When we speak out, we make sure we are heard.
When we want change, we make sure it happens.
When we want happiness, we take it.

But when all else fails, hope remains to guide us to our next challenge.

LUKE ARANDA

Speaking Loud

A powerful message
To everyone
I read this passage

From atop Niagara Falls
To Sutro Tower
Everyone has a voice
And everyone has a choice

Not everyone gets chances
But in the land of the free
Everyone gets a say
From New York to Santa Fe

This country stands tall
A message to you all
You are free
You have a voice
You have a choice

NOEL ATKINSON

Let the Light Shine

Let the light shine, said the sun in the sky,
As the people on earth went about their day.
Little dots on its canvas is how we began.

Consumed by work, we go about our time.
We cross others always, but stay wordless as we go by.
The work of their forefathers standing beside and all around us.
Buildings, brick by brick and trains, track by track.

The fears of the past dormantly await.
People dreading the unknown on an endless path.
Still we can finish our journey together, united.

Wounds of before burn and echo in our ears.
The screams of torment and songs of hope.
The day turned bleak, grim and dark.
While we sit idly by waiting for dawn.

That rise will be soon upon us.
Like that sun in the sky,
All that must be done, is to
Let the light shine.

GRACE BIGELOW-LETH

Swirls of Gold Hope

Gold swirls and twirls of bittersweet,
just beyond the grey horizon.
That is where our hopes lie.
Keeping the dark thoughts away.
They will be achieved someday.

Each of us with our own journey.
Here is where our paths meet.
I dream of traveling to New York City.
Seeing buildings wrapped in snow blankets of warmth,
families gathered around fires,
catching snowflakes on my tongue.

Like footsteps, our journeys will cross.
In our reunions,
we combine our own knowledge with that of others.

Alone, an award winning scientist at NASA will not fix the
    environment.
Alone, the girl in the seat next to you on the bus will not cure world
    hunger.
Alone, the cashier at Safeway will not make the United States equal for
    everyone.
Together, these people could change our world.

There are many strengths of the United States.
We are educators, learners,
pioneers, dreamers.

Flaws occupy our population as well.
They may be overlooked,
but remain just as influential.

A storm known to all as Climate Change
brings clouds to cover our beautiful horizon.
Like Hurricane Katrina,
Climate Change brings with it darkness and demise.

Together, though, we can work to help our planet.
Race, gender, religion,
wealth, political stance-
all factors that do not affect a person's ability to contribute.
Not when the place humans have lived on for 200,000 years is in
    danger.

There will be significant losses to accompany the victories.
That flaming scarlet you see mixed in the horizon,
it pays tribute to lives lost.
But the gold—
The golden swirls represent the plethora of lives saved.
The future generations thanking us,
for giving them a chance at a future.

CONNER BLACK

A Year...

A year of pain.
A year of sorrow.
Pushing forward and barely holding on.
Understanding that what we once knew is gone.
Seeing all we've known crumble down.
Feeling as if we might drown.
Fires raging through our home.
Leaving us on our own.
Wrongful killing of those who care.
A burden their families should never have to bear.
Loved ones dying that we can't save.
Hoping, praying, they'll be ok.
Fighting through the hardships for ourselves and those who fear.
Knowing we can't be close but in our hearts we'll still be near.
With all the pain and all the sorrow.
We come together to build a better tomorrow.
A year of compassion.
A year of unity.
People who come together in the street.
To put up a hand and march to one beat.
To object the wrong that has been done.
The death of a boy who was simply on a run.
The death of a woman in her own home, safe not even there.
The death of a man who was not given the right to a single breath of air.
People have come together.
To stand with one another.
Firefighters who go through all these pains,
in order to stop the raging red flames.
Scientists who have stayed up day and night,
to come up with a way to end this bitter fight.
Healthcare workers who risk their lives to save others.
To save our mothers, fathers, sisters, brothers.
And you, who have given up so much.
Even the comfort of one another's touch.
All of whom our heroes.
Heroes who were always there but now are springing to light.
A nation coming together to combat this horrific fight.
The beauty of our country and everyone in it.
To improve ourselves, to improve each other, to improve our nation.

BRIAN BOOHER

Everyday

Everyday is different although it feels like a routine.
Everyday is full of opportunity and new experiences.
Everyday is another day to live and be free.
Everyday is a day to believe in the American dream.
Everyday is a time we can thank and appreciate those who keep us safe.
Everyday is a chance to mend broken bonds.
Everyday is a chance to forgive and remember.

These next years will be different although it may feel like a routine.
These next years will be full of opportunity and new experiences.
These next years will be years to live and be free.
These next years will be years to believe in the American dream.
These next years we can thank and appreciate those who keep us safe.
These next years will be full of chances to mend broken bonds.
These next years we can forgive and remember.

As this seems to be true for the present and the future,
It wasn't always like this in the past.
Our country was built on blood and tears,
Of people who faced prejudice for years and years.
We must remember them and their history,
So that we will work together to better our future.
For America is full of diversity,
This diversity has turned us against each other in the past;
But this diversity should unite each other in the future and the present

MAYA BOYSEN

After Miller Williams

We have memorized America,
                    who we have been and where.
In   silence we say the words,

                              why, and who?

But how do we fashion the future?

The children. The children.
With waving hands
and flowering faces.

                    one people
Who dreamed for every child an even chance

Who have seen learning struggle

We know what we have done and   said,

                    all we have tried to become —
just and compassionate, equal, able, and free.
All this in the hands of children,

but looking through their eyes, we can see
what   may come to be.

CAMRYN BYE

A Better Tomorrow

Hear the noise of the sizzling bacon on the stove
The sound the ball makes as it hits the bat at McCovey cove
The stomp of the foot on the cold cement, walking to work
The American people, each uniquely their own
My grandma, an immigrant from Denmark
Embarked on a journey looking for the American dream
A beam of hope for endless opportunities
Making a life of her own that led to the life I have today
That led to me being an American citizen, one day being able to vote
Being able to voice my opinion and search for my own opportunities
A country so divided beginning its journey of being united again
Being guided by a new leader hoping for a better tomorrow
Leaving our sorrow for something better to follow
A better tomorrow is a world with no racism
Where everyone can feel safe in their own skin
Where everyone can feel uniquely their own without feeling judged
That would be a win, a better tomorrow
Now that we have finally found some light
I hope it continues to burn bright

ELEANOR CARPENTER

Inaugural Poem

From mac & cheese to salads
From playing house to buying one
From picking off the olives to eating them first
From playing dress up to putting on makeup
From princess dresses to suits
We grow up
Not from good to bad
Nor from old to new
From what was to what is
From what fit then to what fits now
Driven by hope
We adapt
We learn
We grow
And we keep growing even
When it's uncomfortable
When it's ugly
When it's unknown
From child to adult
From colonies to a nation
From owned to free
From war to peace
From silenced to screaming
And now we face another growth spurt
One that aches in our knees
pains our backs
Thrusts us endlessly forward; never reaching the end
Leaving us taller
From mac & cheese to salads
From what was to what is
From child to adult
From divided to united

DEVON CHANEY

Space

What is Space to us but stars that glow
An escape from our problems and disgrace
Or maybe for some a brighter tomorrow
For millennia humans have gazed above
In amazement and wonder
When we look at the Stars with love
Remember, they are the same stars our ancestors lived under
The same Northern Star that many followed to freedom under chase
The same Moon that Apollo took us to
The same sky where the Challenger Disaster took place
The same space where beyond our Solar System lies Voyager 2
And soon we will return to the Moon and visit Mars united as a nation
Guided by our American spirit of exploration
To explore new worlds is our mission
And begin this new age of exploration

ABIGAILE CO

We the People

We the people,
do not succumb,
as a blessing or a curse,
since the birth of our nation,
we the people,
do not succumb,
Embarking with the Revolution,
The patriots did not succumb to the redcoats,
The Donner-Reed Party did not succumb to the numbing cold,
Parks did not succumb to racism,
But all for what you may ask,
What possible reason would be responsible for all the countless
sacrifices made,
What made the 54th regiment keep running towards the face of death,
What made Martin Luther King stand up to the racist threats,
What made Michael Jordan keep pushing when he was told a reinjury
to his foot would separate him from basketball,
The answer is drive,
Drive for passion,
Drive for love,
Drive for proving something or someone wrong or right,
Drive is inside of everyone,
Republican, Democrat, female, male, White, Black, Asian, Hispanic,
straight, gay, bi,
It's all in us,
Some people just might have to find it,
Now what's the future has in store,
It's truly unforeseeable,
There are a billion paths someone could take,
But the good part is that it's up to you,
Up to us,
The only thing we cannot do is let our differences get between us,
Whether democrat or republican, we are still Americans,
We cannot fall too in favor of one side,
George Washington warned us about this in his farewell address,
We must take in what Washington said and apply it to ensure we do not
self destruct our own nation,
We, the people, decide the future of America.

ALLISON CO

Untitled

Day to day we tend to our affairs,
Strolling towards fulfillment,
We reveal our voice.

We start the day with the cold air,
I hear the quiet whisper of the wind,
I listen to the bombastic waves thunder,
And the harbor bell sing.

We open our computers,
We see the dull faces of our acquaintances,
We listen to our teachers,
We unmute to speak.

When my eyes meet the screen,
I stare, the big red exit button a click away,
I listen, the educator describes the assignment,
I learn, the mind pays attention.

We use to roam the halls,
Stare at the white boards,
Listen to the lecture,
Engage in the Labs.

We use to pursue activities,
She shot the basketball,
He hit the baseball,
They played their instruments.

When will those days come back to us,
When will these days end?

Winter comes, the vaccine arrives.
Will the nightmare end, or begin.

Will we celebrate, with joyous cheer,
Or mourn in deep sorrow?

During this time of crises,
Some toil away,
Some hide under rocks,
Some overindulge,
Some resist.

We lie here now,
Unable to thrive in the life we used to call normal.

We don't get to see what happens in the future,
but many things can stay the same.
Your competitive streak,
The love you share,
Your determination and ambition.

At the end of the day,
I hear the quiet whisper of the wind,
I listen to the bombastic waves thunder,
And the harbor bell sing.

TREVOR CORUCCINI

Wake Up

Wake up, work hard, go to bed, repeat,
Living with these ideals gives me worries for future generations,
Having all these pressures makes everyone feel incomplete,
Not having a direction in life gives us no destination.
Leaving the good old days before we knew it,
In the bubble we live in we start to see a haze,
Wondering when we are going to admit,
That we are possibly in the last of our days.
Unless where are able to unite,
We must solve our needs before our wants,
We cannot go down without a fight,
Everyone needs to figure out a response.
We must start to think faster,
Vaccines seem to be the only worry,
But patience is an art we are yet to master,
We can't make everything in a hurry.
People are continuously becoming sick,
We shall wake up, solve problems, work together, and repeat,
If need to make sure everything begins to click,
Or else, we will have to accept defeat.

RONIT DAS

Life Inside

Living inside
Can't travel far or wide
Class is distanced
Life is getting lanced
Maybe a short walk in between
Only seeing friends on screen
People taking too much
Others not doing such
People staying apart
Others get too close, not very smart
People staying away from those sick
Others must bravely help those
And I am grateful.
Life inside.

BELA DAVILA

Days

Days will walk by.
They may stop to say,
"Have a nice day."
Though sometimes they may,
shed a tear into your way,
when all that was needed,
was an embrace,
and some time to be away.
To be away from entanglements in your busy mind.
To be away from the happenings of a glitched nation.
To be away from the people, telling you what is wrong.
The days may bring anger, happiness, disgust, grief, confusion, regret,
    excitement, love, hatred,
Fear.
Fear of what is to come and what needs to get done.
Fear that another innocent life can be lost.
Fear that the future cannot be guessed.
Relief.
A feeling desired,
wanted.
A break-free,
from worry, weighing on the mind.
A feeling so many long for,
for at least one time,
during the year that has failed to grant the wishes and the hopes of
    those who so bravely told themselves, that this year,
would be theirs.
As days have brought us grief, confusion and wonder of what is to
    come,
time has approached to the colder moments of our year,
the moments in between.
The moments when everyone gets to make their voice heard,
to be a part of something,
even for a second.
Days of relief.
When the correct answer can be heard by all.
Days of happiness,
because everyone deserves their rights.
Days that won't bring the fear of another tragedy.

Days worry free.
Days that bring relief.
Days free, from fear.

HANNAH DE LEON

It Belongs to the Brave

"The future doesn't belong to the fainthearted; it belongs to the brave."
—Ronald Reagan

When you think of the
word change what do you think of, the future
good things, the bad, the possibility to create something greater, doesn't
it makes you wonder why we aren't at our full potential, why some still
    feel like they don't belong

To me it means something much deeper, the opportunity to
learn and improve from whatever comes your way, and the
opportunity to take the steps to make a difference, however this isn't a
    task for the fainthearted

to improve ourselves, our society, our country, it
is up to the people who make others feel like they belong
even in a world where others are not accepting, and to
make the unaccepting become open to and supportive of the idea of
    change, it is up to the people who are willing to take that step and
    break that wall, it is up to the brave

ALLI DIOLI

The Day That Changed Everything

It was one day in December,
the year 2019 we found out about Covid-19.
Not much was said, not much was known.
It wasn't until March 2020 that we stepped up.
We stepped up for the better of America,
Because that is what we do for our country.
That one day started the confusion, the questions,
the hope that this will be over.
That one day started the strive for an even better
and stronger America.
America has pushed through the 1918 pandemic.
We see ourselves pushing through Covid.
Doing our part as Americans, as equals, is
to listen to the science so that we can see loved
ones, go to work, go to school, and live our lives without
the fear of losing more people to this virus.
Covid is not going to go walking.
We need to step forward, because covid
made its way in.
We can fix that.
At the end of the tunnel there is light.
That one day will soon be long gone in our memories.

DREW DORWIN

Chaos.

Chaos that surrounds us, all around us, all the time, like a powerful Army around a lone soldier.

Chaos, that discriminates us, separates us, boiling the minds of people who tirelessly beg, and scream for change.

The small pull of a finger on a trigger that tears us apart, with only a hope of reunion

A dream of peace and Justice.

The American dream—a fantasy soft by many, but only a lost dream now, hoping to recover

through this new beginning.

But hope beckons.

Change is inevitable, yelling at our people, like a teacher getting the attention of a class.

The struggle for equality, that we beg for, hoping to be brought to an end in this new era.

People working hard, harder, endlessly, working for a change for happiness in a race with not one winner but with three hundred million glorious first place trophies.

Recovery of a once-great Nation, recovery from a broken promise that lied to us saying it would make us great.

But now we have hope, brought on by us, America, us, by our citizens.

You can see it in our eyes, the hope mixed with the anticipation, gleaming in people's faces, a light that shines, powered collectively by our souls.

An optimism that hopes to Stray From Fear. An optimism that hopes to stray from its past evils and learn from them, and rebuild into a giant towering skyscraper. An optimism that fights fire with the fire in the hearts of all the hard-working Americans, in this newborn leadership of Biden and Harris.

COCO DUBOSE

A New Chapter, We Begin.

We begin to learn, grow and thrive, but this time together.
America smiles for its first time in four years.
Waiting to chop down the rotten tree and plant the new one.
    Impatiently we sit waiting for the long overdue change.
Hand in hand, heart on sleeve.
Could this be the change we need? Will it change it all?
We may sit here not knowing what the future can hold, but we sit here
    together, as Americans.

COLE ECKERT

Life

Life is wonderful.
It brings people joy and happiness.
It gives us amazing experiences.
Life is a wild ride full of highs, but also lows

With life comes hardship.
Times of hurt and pain.
Destruction and loss.
Last year was one of those times.

Life bit us humans in the back.
Life woke us up from our fantasies and brought us into reality.
Life is trying to tell us it is a time for change.
And yet humans still refuse to listen.

We must wake up and rise.
If we wish to get ourselves out of the hole that we have dug ourselves
    into.
We shall remember this time in the future.
So we don't make the same mistakes.

The next years will be times of repair, of improvement.
Of upbringing and hope.
We must all work together to achieve this better future.
Work hard to fix the damage that has been done

Take this new year as a clean slate.
A new period of opportunities, and new experiences.
Take this as a time for the betterment of yourself.
And others around you.

Let's all stand together as one to solve this problem.
To fix the problems of our past and the potential problems of our
    future.
We cannot be the blue states and red states.
We must set aside our differences and be the United States.

MIA ETHERIDGE

A Garden Grown in Wisdom

Today, tomorrow, and the day after that, a garden will grow
A garden of life and death
of great opportunity and of great failure
A garden where you can die in the soil
or sprout through the concrete

We are the Garden of Eden
We live peacefully until the curious ones arrive
Some want to eat the apple
Some would rather not
Pioneers are hungry
Followers would rather starve

We all must bite the apple
and learn to build something better
Learn to unite and to dissolve
Learn to educate and to teach
Learn to love and to care
To teach our children knowledge from wisdom
For they will be the designers of the future and the successors of
    history

We all must bite the apple
And learn to live with it

Learn to grow a new garden from apple seeds

NORA FLYNN

Grass

Cement and brick
Dead leaves crack under my weary feet
My shoes scuff along the cracked sidewalk
Where there once was grass

The sidewalk in the city is narrow
It smells of gas and rain
A wilted maple hangs under the dusty sky
A cigarette butt at its base
Where there once was grass

A field of corn, young, green and tall
Waves before me
Before it is stripped from its stalk
To be sold
Now brown husks lay on the dirt
Where there once was grass

A field is full of tiny men
The white and red of the flag wave in the wind against the blue
An endless roar arises as jets fly overhead
Filling the air with smoke and remembrance
Its sickly sweet fumes descend upon the crowd
I cough
The metal bleachers clang as I move away
Towards where there once was grass

The fluorescent lights blind me
The store is filled with shiny mounds of colored fruits
They topple from their stands like dropped beads
They stop rolling against my feet
On cold plastic tile
Where there once was grass

There is fog and quiet
My car would hum as it rolled along the road
It stopped
The air is cool and clear
The smell of salt is sharp

Tiny pieces of history moved beneath me as I walked towards the
    empty ocean
There is no grass here
There never was
There is only rock and salt and water
It no longer smells of salt
It smells of gas
And fish
There are bottle caps and plastic knives
Boats line the horizon
The ocean is full
A crowded picnic area stretches to the water
I walk over the bright green turf, the plastic bits sticking to my toes
There is grass here

LILY FORTIN

The Voices

The world is still.
The sun rises to greet the clouds.
The clouds wrap their loving arms around the sun as if to welcome it.

All around us people move.
The world is still yet bursting with movement.
As we greet the day, some earlier than others.

We all walk side by side.
Down the busy sidewalks.
People standing anxiously waiting for something.

However separate we gather as one.
We gather to soak in the knowledge of another.
The people who speak of hope and a new day.

From the ground our ancestors built the world we are chained to.
The world we live in.
They worked for us to work harder.

The dirt which we rub off our shoes others have planted seeds in.
These seeds are the small but mighty ones of this world.
The seeds of workers and dreamers.

We gather together yet apart.
We listen as one and as many.
The thoughts in which we hear fill our own ears.

As we listen closely we hear the words of others.
We gather as one yet we are so different.
We learn to live and work in this world as one.

We listen for our future.
Our family, our children.
We listen for the years to come.

We are the citizens, the people, the voices.
We gather together to make a decision to choose a leader.
The one to walk fearlessly as a leader.

JORDAN GIRARD

Everything is Okay

Rainy day
In a deep dark abyss
In my own mind
Millions of thoughts tangled up
Glancing at the peaceful streets
I do not feel peaceful
This overwhelming feeling controlling my body
Just breathe
In
1 2 3
Out
1 2 3
Am I real
I am a crashing wave
In this peaceful ocean
In
1 2 3
Out
1 2 3
We spend our lives
Chasing for happiness
Avoiding what is right in front of us
In
1 2 3
Out
1 2 3
I need to appreciate the moment
Putting all bad aside
Feeling okay again
In
1 2 3
Out
1 2 3
I am still
I am now calm like the rest of the ocean
Everything is okay

ELIJAH GJOVIG

Untitled

In the past, America was divided
In the present, we are getting better
In the future, we'll stand united
So much anger and hate in this country
America is at a crossroads

It was written in our countries founding documents that everyone is
    created equal
But this hasn't been the case
So much pain and suffering in the past
Still, so much progress to be made
There is far too much hate

The last four years have been exhausting
But there's hope for the future
We're still not where we should be
But slowly getting there
America is at a crossroads

KAIA GLAFKIDES

America Today

When you're eight years old
You don't think about
The world melting away
Or people dying because of the color of their skin
Picking cotton, How far have we come?
Hungry and without a home
At recess
Playing, while another school is under attack
Are our fathers being torn from our families?

Afraid to walk alone at night
Because I am a female
One thousand and thirty nine killed at the hands of police
Relentless.
Boys will be boys… just ruining lives
Why are children still starving?
White supremacy concealed but malicious
Nobody is illegal on stolen land

Hanging heavy
Together, we can overcome our ceaseless issues

SCARLETT GLAZEBROOK

Death by the People

We used to be able to breathe the air provided
Sealife used to be able to swim freely
The ocean used to be just salt water
We used to be able to predict what is to come each season

Now the world is melting everyday
Now backs are turned so more can be earned
Now the ocean has turned black from oil spills
Now sealife mistake plastic for food
Now air is ruined for personal achievements
Now fires blaze everywhere, scorching the nation
Now heat rays combusting the land for miles, destroying families and
    dreams
Now increasingly intense water and winds drenching and drowning
    people
Now down on the poles ice is chipping away

The earth has become a ticking time bomb
Henceforth the world should start healing
The earth should be put first
Earnings and achievements should come after the welfare of mother
    nature
The ones that have the power refuse to share it
This destruction started with the people and should be ended by the
    people

ALEXA GODOY

Untitled

We wake up and brush our teeth,
We head out to work,
To buildings to homes to gardens and schools,
Go about our lives.
While some of us wake up in fear,
We worry about what will happen to us next
Watching stories on the news
Seeing innocent people getting killed
Seeing innocent people getting blamed
Why do we have to live this way?
Why do we have to live in fear?
Where is the equality?
We live in America
A place filled with dreams
A place that shouldn't have fear
We need each other
We need to come together as one
Where is "with liberty and justice for all"?

JACOB GOLDSTEIN

Untitled

Each droplet is free to move
independently
A storm brews and droplets clash
Some droplets drift
carried apart in a spray
Others form a wave for justice
A great noise for the oceans ear
Endless waves crash on our shores
A rhythmic pound forever beating
Sometimes strong and powerful
Other times quiet and serene
A wave rises up high
A wave barely crashes
Each droplet combines making a great sea
The water moves together
One entity
one nation
Our waves pound the shore
Shaping sands of tomorrow

VALERIA LOPEZ GONZALEZ

Fear

We all live in fear, we live in America.
We get up and get ready for the day.
We go to work, in fear,
We go to school, in fear,
And out we go, into the world, in fear.
Everywhere we go, we go in fear.

Why do people have fear and live in fear?
Isn't America supposed to be the dream land?

On the news we see people get killed for no reason.
We see people get called racial slurs,
We see people get criticized because of their sexuality,
And all of that just because of the color of their skin, their religion, or
who they love.

Isn't America supposed to be the place that people dream of living in?
And isn't a dream place supposed to be a safe and a good environment?
Then why do all of us consistently live in fear?

IRIS GRANT

Land of the Free

Land of the Free
One of the first words you think of when you hear America
But not everyone was free
The America then was full of hate
Full of discrimination
People murdered for their race or sexuality
And as they began to accept themselves
Society shut them out
Kids forced to attend segregated schools
And forced to grow up in a dying society

The America now is full of anger
Anger which causes riots
Anger which causes mass shootings
And innocent people getting murdered

The America in the future has hope
Hope which brings acceptance.
Hope which brings improvement.
Hope which brings a light at the end of the tunnel

Nothing is born perfect
And all beautiful things must be worked for
A flower can't grow without water
A tree needs to sprout to grow apples
And a baby can't be born without love

We make the choices
We decide who we want to be
As a whole we need to do better
Start a new chapter
Together

KAYLANI GUEVARA

Untitled

The America then was full of hate
Full of discrimination and power struggle
Plantation workers and cotton pickers
Men and women lynched and killed for no good reason
Children not allowed to learn in fear of them being educated
An endless cycle of darkness
Surrounding the lives of those who were never really sure of what went
 wrong
Never understood why they were treated the way they were
But this was considered the "land of the free," right?

The America now is full of hate
Innocent people getting murdered
Allowing candy bars to be guns
Allowing 20 years of jail to be death penalties
Allowing speeding tickets to be murder
Heads turning away from the problem
Pretending they don't see what's right in front of them
Chipping away at equality
America is not making any progress
But we have the most funding for military services in the world, right?

The America in the future has hope
As a whole we need to do better
Climb the Rocky Mountains
Instead of just looking at the hill
Plant the flower in the garden
Instead of letting the weeds grow
We can't stay paused in time
Start a new chapter
Together

America can be beautiful
No matter the race of its people
America is full of working hands
No matter the sexuality of its people
America is full of busy minds
No matter the gender of its people
America is full of creative thoughts

No matter the religion of its people
Opportunity for all

This is our America
We make the choices
We decide who we want to be
Nothing is born perfect
All beautiful things must be worked for
The bald eagle needs to learn to fly before it can hunt
The tree needs to sprout before it can grow apples
A still lake needs just one rock
To start a movement across the whole body of water
Our America has its rock
Let's start our movement

KAIYA HANEPEN

We Must Restore the Soul of America

—After Joe Biden's Victory Speech (November 7th, 2020)
& Elizabeth Alexander's "Praise Song for the Day"

We must restore the soul of America. **I**
will spare no effort, none, or any commitment to turn around this
    pandemic. We can do it. I **know**
we can. **There's**
never been anything we've not been able to do when we've done it
    together. **Something**
will happen. Our country will achieve **better**.
America will grow and not be held **down**.
It's a task, **the**
task of our time. The **road**
there is clear. We must restore the soul of America.

LIAM HARRINGTON

Untitled

We sit here gathered, wondering what the future will hold, America.
The land of opportunity.
The one who works hard, plays hard, and achieves hard. Each step has
a landmark, a story behind it. Each different person with no same story
and no same past. As we sit here looking at the new rock of our
country, our new anchor holding us down together. A new story to
begin, in a new chapter of our lives. Waiting for what's to come we
stand strong and together as Americans, all different races and religions,
but Americans. Americans, the no founding definition that keeps
changing, just like our country. So we sit here. Proud to be Americans.

RYAN HARRINGTON

Untitled

America, the land of many views
Different people, different stories, different religions all in one country,
We sit here together waiting,
Looking at our new hope for the future.
Our chance for a fresh start,
A new hope that stands by our flag.
Could this be it?
The new chance we have been longing for.
As we sit wondering
We put our faith in our country.
The rock holding us down,
The rock keeping us together.

HAILEY HERNANDEZ

High School

A place where you're supposed to meet new people
Make new friends
Talk in the hallways
Listen to your teachers
Do homework

But instead we are at home
We get up and log onto our computers
We sit patiently while we wait
Wondering when this class will end
How much longer

We repeat the process over and over again
We sit patiently
Waiting for school to end

Then school is over
We take a break
We eat
We breathe
And prepare ourselves for homework

Homework takes hours
Hours of stress
Hours of hardship
Hours of rummaging through our notes trying to find an answer to our
    question

We take breaks throughout the night
Then we go back and continue working
We finish late at night at finally turning in our assignments before the
    clock strikes 12
And start all over again the next day

KAY HILDEBRAND

America

America,
The dream, the vision, the promised land.
But is that really true?

America,
Land of the free, home of the brave.
Where all men are created equal.
But are ALL people really treated equally?

America,
The place where dreams come true,
Where people can build their new lives in a safe environment,
But is it really safe for everyone?

No.
America isn't what everyone says it to be.
America isn't the dream for everyone,
America is the dream for white men.

Yes,
America is the land of the free,
and the home of the brave.

No.
All men are not created equally.
Women are not seen as equal to men.
Blacks, Hispanics, Latinos, Asians, and other minorities are not treated
    as equals to whites.

Yes.
America can be the place where your biggest dreams come true.
Most Americans have the opportunity to build their new lives in a safe
    environment,
But not all Americans.

America is built on a set of ideals.
America can live up to its expectations as soon as we fight to meet
    those ideals.

America isn't there yet.
But we can be.

We are America.
We hold the power to change these issues.
We can make this the land of the free, where all people are treated
    equally.
But we have to work together.

CALLIE HOFFMAN

Land of the Free

Land of the Free.
One of the first words you think of when you hear America.
But it makes you wonder
Who is free?
Not the people murdered for their race or sexuality.
Not the youth growing up in a dying world.
Not the people separated from their family and put in cages.

America has a lot of anger.
Anger which causes riots.
Anger which causes mass shootings.
Anger which causes families not to speak to each other.

America has a lot of love.
Love which lets people see the good in things.
Love which lets people empathize.
Love which lets families reunite.

America has a lot of hope.
Hope which brings acceptance.
Hope which brings improvement.
Hope which brings a light at the end of the tunnel.

America has all of these things.
This is what makes it so special.
It has the tools to grow and rebuild.
Even with all of the dark shadows of our past and present,
Our hope for the future illuminates the bright path ahead.
Land of the free.

ANASOFIA INFANZON-MARIN

"Say it plain: that many have died for this day."

—After Elizabeth Alexander

I hear the loud whispers of those around me. What they **say**
It seems to mean nothing but carries the weight of the world. **It**
is as if you are forced to hold your breath, hoping the world could stay:
    plain.
With one swoop everything could change instantly, **that**
which everyone found mundane will affect **many**
Ignorance is bliss, people want what those people **have**
The people who see have had to witness suffering and mourn those
    who have **died**
"Justice for all" something most yearn **for**
This year is time to achieve all of it, all of **this**
is riding on this **day**

JADE IRELAND

For All

A country full of hate.
Of discrimination.
We all stand watch,
Just letting it happen.

When will it stop?
When will it end?
When will people stand together,
Hand in hand?
Gay, straight, black, white,
We're all the same,
We're all people.

We'll stand up and fight
Fight for what's right.
And when we fall,
We will only stand again.

We are people,
And we are America.
Together we stand.
One nation
Under God
Indivisible
With liberty and justice
For all.

EMILY JENAR

Untitled

You may not know where to start
There are lots we can do to save this planet
Everyone just needs to do their part

Your teacher may recycle
Your brother may shop sustainable
You could make a difference just by riding your bicycle

Make sure to save your glasses, paper and tin
You can conserve our natural resources
Simply by putting them in the correct bin

The ozone layer is depleting
Make sure to keep seeding
These plants will help our breathing
And do the healing

You can make a difference by making earth clean
reducing, reusing and recycling
All together we can keep it green

JULIAN JIMENEZ

Children of America

America gets tired of all of our fighting.
To her we are her children.
"There is no reason to fight," she says each day.
She wants everything to stop.
But can it? Are we too caught up in the luxury of living in America?
Living in America has its perks but everyday we grow soft.
Everyday we pass on blindly not knowing the bad things in the real
world.
Inside the comfort of our homes we are shielded away from external
harms.
This is not a bad thing though it obstructs our views on a lot of things.
During this pandemic going outside is not accessible.
Which means seeing America to the full extent is difficult.
Try to see the world in a new light.
After all, We are all American.

ANA JOHNSTON

Safer

Under the green leaves I catch my breath
Quiet, soft, gentle the light surround me
Chirps and whistles tickle my soul
The wind touches me
I am safe
The narcissistic voice has been silenced
Ugly souls are not gathering on streets
Rough hands are not grabbing innocent bodies
Pretenders become ghost
We are safer
I sit while smiling with my friends
Laughing at twinkling stars
Hugs not guns
Trust not lies
I am safer
It's too hot to focus on school
Classes are closed due to smoke
Masks cover the smiles we had
Holidays are quiet and less
We need to feel safer

DOMINIC KATOUT

Beauty and Spirit

Days aren't things, but miracles
Past, future and present, it matters not
Failure or success, lore is gained
But to succeed truly, always aim high

The American land, her graceful beauty
Let her shine her freedom fully
We all help each other, even if it's small
We make our lands diverse and share all our love
Love even in its spirit and your hard work
Even when that work becomes spirit, it strings us along

Will you ever slice through your despair?
Or have you already shone through the despair, the bleakness and
    sorrow?

It's as if it were yesterday
When I was small and naive
But thanks to you, you and especially you,
You aimed my spirits high

JOSEPHINE KEARNS

A New Home

Boats in the water, men stepping onto the shore of a new place
A new home, strange and exciting, a new start
More boats in the water, but these do not carry freedom
They carry chains, a future to come of cruelty, labor, and unfairness
Other men are soldiers, fighting for freedom, fighting for change
But when change comes, we are not united
Splitting like a piece of cloth
North from south, white from black, men from women
A new fight for change, for the right to vote, for a seat on the bus

And now, people living and dying in isolation
Millions dead from the pandemic, millions affected
Businesses shut down, children struggling to learn at home
Fires raging from a changing climate
Ice melting, plant and animal species never seen again
Pollution in the water, in the streets, in the air
People in the streets, marching for what they believe in
Fighting against police brutality, fighting to be heard, fighting for
    change

The sun will rise again tomorrow
Approaching a time with a woman leading the country
Voices of different people with different views all heard and considered
Working together to create a sustainable future
Wind turbines turning, trees growing
A healthier planet with a healthier population
Possibilities and dreams for all ages, genders, and colors

ALEX KORON

Untitled

We've all been in the dark for a long time now
Not where you can still feel the moon on your skin
Instead, you're trapped in a room without barriers
Each day is yet another rough patch
Another grind just to make it to bed
Another day with effort just for effort's sake
Everyone just keeps saying,
We're almost there, don't stop now
We're almost there, The light is near
Nobody wants to keep hearing,
We're nearly there, why are you stopping now?
We're nearly there, Can't you see the light?
Yet despite the numerous challenges
The gut punching, unyielding circumstances
The cruel, unfair wrongly placed punishments
We continue to move on, to stand up
To fall down, to be ripped apart
To fly forward, to mend broken wounds
When we were asked, can you keep going?
Can you keep pushing forward?
Can you search for the light when it's nowhere in sight
We stood proud, chin up, eye's set forward shouting,
We won't stay down, We won't stay still
We won't stop now, We will find the light

KAIJA LAAKES

Untitled

In 1776, we gained our independence; a
Long time we bled for our families and our home.
We have been through many hardships, large and
Small. Even today we fight for our rights, a
Fight for peace, a fight for acceptance, a fight for this country.
A better life waited as I got here, and as I should
Be sad, I am happy not to leave,
For I feel not as me, but together as us.
We may be different, but no
Two humans are the same. We have hopes and many more.

ASHLEY LAU

My Everyday Fairy Tale

Home described physically is a particular place;
Often with a price, on a path you can trace
Covered in personal trimming and handmade lace
Millions of stacks of atoms, solid in negative space,
Which encase a bed, maybe a bathroom
Maybe a washer and a sink
A pit stop in your daily life
Of which you don't often think.

But it isn't the place that makes the space,
It's the things in the place that show the caring,
Daring to fill the void you don't realize exist
In the gaps of your heart, when things are amiss:

Like when you need to curl up after a hard day,
When your nettled emotions need to settle and lay,
When you need everyone around you to just go away,
Or when you need to know someone will stay;
When life just isn't going your way,
Or when you need to celebrate the day,

Home is here, and home is there, and home
Is wherever the head and heart are
It has been said but it is true.

Even if the heart beats in another person's chest
Or even if no one understands why it's the best
It's yours, and you have no one to impress
Because home is where you feel least pressed.

And admittedly home doesn't make everything better
It may be a shelter, and a place of work, play and rest
But life will not stop at your behest
There will be fires,
The screaming of tires,
The short circuiting of wires
Parts of the circuitous cycle of life, which uproot homes
Or make you feel helpless.

But just like us, homes are not perfect
Homes are a mirror, a reflection
They can shatter, disappear and scatter
But they are a perfect imperfection
The negatives will come, but they don't seem to matter
Because home is where the heart is
Full of love, full of laughter
Your very own,
Hand tailored,
Mundane happily ever after.

KAI LESTER

Everyone's America

As the eagle sings from a distant shore
Its wings bruised and battered
The eagle tries to fly and soar
Its wings still left tattered.

As the eagle struggles through the air
Crying its song of hope
Its song falls on ears of despair
Their hands tied down in rope.

As a single person rises alone
The huddled masses soon follow
And as a new voice is shown
Their tone changes from one of sorrow.

As the grizzly bear rises from its slumber
Its head once again held high
It treads now unencumbered
As it looks up to the sky.

As the eagle soars in a newfound grace
Finding a new perch up above
Its song now registers as a case
Of one full of hope and love.

As the bear joins the eagle in its song
Letting out its mighty roar
Their voices ring true and strong
And are no longer able to be ignored.

As the crowd now chants from down below
Their voices full of rage
The people from up above now know
That it is time for change.

As everyone's voices are now being heard
Their stories, some from afar
Are told as this country's cure
That begins to heal our scars.

And as the Sun rises on a new day
Now everyone can say
This is my America.

KAI FUJINO LIN

Stars in the Dark Night

2020, the year everything was turned on its head.
Where the dark times have come upon us.
But even in the darkest places is,
Where we see the brightest lights.
The dark year of 2020 for America.
But we as the people of America,
Must shine and make the dark beautiful.
As the stars in the flag,
Are the states in the country.
We must make the Milky Way in the dark night sky.
As more stars in the night shine,
The brighter the night becomes.

JESCENT MARCELINO

Flight

to the unknown

Mesmerized
　　by the lights,
The land
　　blurred by my sight
The moon,
　　I saw day and night
That was all because of a
　　　　　flight.

"We're finally here,"
　　My father murmurs.
A wistful smile etched upon my face
My eyes sparkled with wonder
　　in this foreign new place
Felt the cool dry breeze of the air,
seen the clear celestial sphere
　　I breathe it in,　then out.
the night sky　dark blue
　　as the sun settled in to the pacific,
　　　the ocean　to where I was from.
Twinkling stars from the galaxy above
Weakened by my eyes
　　Hope I can't find

　　The silent noise of people
muttering in different languages
　　incoherent to my ears
　　but proof of my movement

Long lines formed
　　with varying pathways
　　Destinations set on stone
but I'm uncertain on what lies ahead

The moon gleams its light from the warm sun
Though the dark blankets engulf everything
　　Bringing one to fear the unknown

Estranged by everything,
    A greet of disconnection.

The organized placement of lights
  Has given me amazement
    —brought color   to the road ahead
but their distant welcoming
    dulled the vibrancy instead.

This flight to the unknown
  An enigma to my life
A huge obstacle I must trudge on
  A riddle only I could answer.

SADHBH McCLENAGHAN

Means the Toll of a Bell

On past the creek
With its natural flow
Lives the big brown bear
In its natural home.

Into the woods,
Surrounded by trees,
It's a natural climber
On the native Sequoia.

It trudges along,
With pride and with joy,
Its young in its wake,
One dare not destroy.

Some call them grizzlies,
Which may sound ok
But mess with one once,
And you surely will pay.

Their diet is valid,
Berries, leaves, nuts,
They also eat fish,
To fatten their guts.

In winter they hasten,
To dens where they sleep,
You could pass right beside one
And won't hear a peep.

Swimmers and runners,
They do it so well,
If you get to escape one,
What a story you'll tell.

Love them or loathe them,
You have to admit,
How regal, how noble
How incredibly fit.

So take heed of my story,
And mind yourself well,
For a bear on your six,
Means the toll of a bell!

SYDNEY MCGUIRK

Tense and Time

Today is today,
Tomorrow is tomorrow,
We are in the present,
Not the past or future,
Let us not look back but forward,
Learn from the past as they say,
Accept your losses and go home,
Peel off the helmet,
Say congratulations,
And return home putting on a mask to protect yourself from the past,
Not us, Not today,

We embrace and do not hide,
We look to the past to honor those before us,
The men and women,
With sweat beaded bodies,
Strength like my fathers,
And calloused hands,
Scared with memories,
Storybooks,
They all tell stories of the past,
Where you come from,
Who you are,
It might be critical but it does not define you,
You are what makes this wheel turn,
The decisions made,
They define us,
This is our decision for the future,
What happens now defines it,

We are often asked who you are,
To that the answer is I don't know,
We will never truly know who we are for our story is never ending,
Instead stand for something,
Shout scream
Walk run
And all of the above
Never stop telling your story,

What do you see in the future?
Truth Loyalty Love Power,
Let your voice be heard,
I see a river flowing letting all things bad pass like a changing of the
  tide,
I see a rock solid as the power we hold,
I see a tree grounding us into our roots,

In the present I feel trapped,
I hope for a life living outside the box,

So take a moment,
Drop the mask,
And uncover what is in front of you,
For this is the past, present, and future.

MADISON MELO

Change

The sun rises and sets every day
Often those go on with their day without looking around at the world
Changes are happening
Not just to those around us but to our home
Changes need to be made
Climate change is real
White privilege is real
Racism is real
Often people look past these problems because they don't affect them
Those who are looked at differently need to be heard
Our mother earth needs to be heard
Us people need to change
Ice caps are melting
Sea levels are rising
Drastic temperature changes
But people still don't believe it's real
Change needs to be made in this world
People need to look at what is going on in the world now
We all need to make a change in our lives
This world is not what it used to be

MAKALA MESINA-FORESTER

The Song of Today

A song plays this day.
It's carried by the wind.
Blowing past our ears.
If you stop and listen, you will hear it.
Most people don't.
Quietly playing as it has been for generations.
This song can be beautiful.
We strain our ears to listen.
Humming it to ourselves as it fades out of mind.
But a song this long has flaws.
Its melodies covered with deep scars and cuts.
The notes jagged and rough.
The song that plays today is weak.
The tune is frail, ready to break.
But a sad song won't remain.
An endless song learns to heal itself.
With the hands of composers.
Willing to listen.

MOSS MICHELSEN

Untitled

Through bravery and might, we won the fight, to secure the land of
    dreams.
A place, a home, where freedom is the name of our nation's tome.
Ten truths were written, to guide the way, for peoples to come, to rid
    our nation of disarray.
In this day, the divide grows stronger, between red and blue, who fight
    and squander.
But piercing this storm, is the realization, that both red and blue are a
    part of this nation.

Dare we crumple this work to the ground. No. We shall take this
    endeavor upon ourselves.
A worthy goal, to uphold this country, to let it stand as a beacon of
    light, in these troubling times.
Like the eye of a storm, our new leader shall be. Stability. The mark of
    a great reader.
So rejoice, for new beginnings sing, for our nation as a whole, and the
    individual.
Together, we stand, looking forward, looking, standing, us together.

OWEN MILLER

America, A Country in Pain

As an American it is your right to be happy
when we wake up we put a smile on our face and walk out the door
Under that fake smile is a person suffering the cruelty of this world
Yet, the saying "fake it until you make it" is one that holds true in our
  daily lives

Fake happiness, false hope that all the bad things will just go away
Because with any light there is always shade, when the light fades you
  are left with darkness
Sorrow is unavoidable, pain inevitable and our scared, dark past
  inescapable
It has been a long painful road, with many bright spots and many
  mistakes to learn from and improve on

Our future is bright with lots to look forward to for us to attain the
  prize of happiness
The everpresent pain and suffering of all remains lurking in the
  shadows
A shame really, we long for a goal that seems unattainable and the only
  thing coming to us is unbearable pain
Alas, we can make the light brighter, by punching hard to reach out
  goals and attain peace

Yet here and now, we struggle through daily life, hoping for the best yet
  receiving the worst
In this day and age, for what has felt like an endless cycle of minor
  improvements followed by horrific fails
We look for the good in life, and try to change what is broken to help
  build our national sense of equality and happiness
There is little to look forward to now, yet we still fixate our vision on it
  as to not lose our way and go insane

Fake it until you make it, awful advice that we blindly follow not
  knowing where we are going nor our destination
Fake smiles are on all of us, we are all suffering inside no matter if it's
  miniscule or immeasurable
False hope your phony smile will bring true satisfaction
Yet as an American, it's our right to pursue happiness as we please, so
  we follow this road in the hopes we reach our goal

86

RILEY MILLS

America

America is red
And sparkly, like the shoes of the little girl down the street.

The combination of hardwork and hope make America
Just like the combination of orange and yellow make red.

Americans are sparkles
Each one distinct and autonomous
Contributing to the beautiful red color that is America.

America is also blue
Some people don't believe red and blue can mix
But I think purple is a beautiful color.

I feel that right now America is orange and yellow, not red
Separated
But that's nothing a little paintbrush can't fix.
America is a rainbow

ALESSANDRA MORALES

A Time for Change

We took our chances.
We risked what we had.
But for what?

Many died.
Many tried.
And in the end, we succeeded.
But succeeded in what?

Our ancestors roll in their graves
at the thought of what we've done.

The Civil Rights Act of 1964 gave us what we needed.

De jure segregation was finally rid of our nation.
Yet, we stubbornly held onto de facto.

There's an opportunity to change.
Reverse our habits.
Rewrite our mistakes.
Make Martin proud.
Equality yearns for the attention of our nation.
Yet, we continue to neglect it.
Undoing the work that many strived to accomplish.

BELINDA MORALES

Through My Eyes

As I watch the world through my eyes I wonder,
How did we get here?
I should be enjoying my teenage years
but instead I am shedding tears in fear of what's to come.
Of what's to come in my future.
I know I am not alone on this
as I see people struggling to pay rent,
struggling to bring food for their children to eat,
struggling to keep on working even though they are beat.
I sometimes wonder,
How will we ever recover from this?
How will we dig ourselves up from the hole we entrapped ourselves in?
Now this may seem like an impossible task
but all I ask is for us to come together as a whole
because we all share the responsibility of this big role.
This role of picking up our nation and putting the pieces back together.
This role that should keep us united, not divided.
I know that when we come together we will have hope to bring us
    forward
to be the greatest country anyone has ever seen.
So today I ask you,
hold on to the hope that brings us closer because we will walk into the
    light together.

ELLE MORRIS

There Was Once a Sunrise,

Gold and peach and a dusty dark mauve color
It showed new beginnings, as the faint memories of the night before
lingered on the edges like burnt paper curling inwards,
Memories,
The cold,
The dark,
The uncertainty
But what got you through night was memories of sunbaked skin
Of progress, knowing we are headed in the right direction
And of hope for a new morning
Another chance to regroup and push through
The sun goes down slowly, sometimes so gradually that you don't even
notice it until it's dark and cold and too late to find your way home.
But yet, sometimes the sun is down fast, falling through the sky like it
can wait to play tag with you, not knowing that you can't run after it
But either way America has gotten to a sunrise
And I have faith that this will be its brightest day yet.

MADI MULLINS

Untitled

From the Pacific,
To the Atlantic,
From the Sierra,
To the Valley by the name of death,
From the blazing tropics,
To the snowcapped mountains,
America holds diversity,
Along with beauty beyond compare,
Although it may hold many beauties,
America houses many unresolved topics,

A sound that mirrors fireworks,
May feel protection to some,
Takes form as grim reaper to others,
Fills the graveyards with bones,
With no sign of war,

Snowy mountains rapidly evaporating,
Only this time not at fault of the springtide,
A much more long term summer,
This time not by nature,
This summer is man-made,

Many murdered,
Not as a form of justice,
But for a different reason,
The color of their skin,
Many in America,
Yet again split,
By the cry for Human Rights,

Issues such as these,
Are splitting Americans apart,
We must come to a resolution,
Before these issues cause war,
But this war would be different,
It would be Americans,
Against their fellow Americans,

From the Pacific,
To the Atlantic,
From the Sierra,
To the Valley by the name of death,
From the blazing tropics,
To the snowcapped mountains,
America holds diversity,
Along with beauty beyond compare,
We must unite to keep this beauty,
From turning to despair,

With all the diversity,
We all keep one thing in common,
We are Americans.

SOFIA NADEAU

Exigent

Once rivaled now considered equal,
the oppressed stood.
Stood in memory of those before them,
In remembrance of their ancestors who
endured pain, suffering, and strife.
Stood with their worth and basic human rights up
to the polished, unscathed feet of the commander,
and demanded change.

Change was given, but with uncertainty and hesitancy.
Change was given, but was it truly made?

We say with certainty things have changed.
Things have gotten better.

But look at what's happened.
Our so-called protectors took the life of an innocent man.
I can't breathe.

Our so called protectors took the life of an innocent protector.
Wrong house.

Actions beyond reason.

Lives lost beyond morality

Say their names.

Just as the petals of hope were withering away,
A ray of sun,
A drop of water,
And the revival of aspirations.
Americans were waking up.
Waking up to the cries for justice,
Waking up to the masses marching in the street.
We found our voice and grabbed it as tight as we could.
Because if we didn't, it would slip back into the hands of the
    oppressors.

What is it that we look to?
A fresh page?
A solution?
A cure?
As we look towards the light at the end of the tunnel, we look for a
    resolution.
Look.

Merely looking is not nearly enough.

We mustn't stand in the rushing rapids yearning to get across.
Standing will only allow the rapids to push you back.
Move forward.
Push back.
Stand tall.

Nature is beckoning.
Nature is exigent, demanding for motion.

AKHILENDRA NAIR

The Tyranny of Repetition

America
As we witness the coming year, We discern in our grief
Among the clamor of objection, the cries for righteousness
Pain, hardship, and prejudice in the land of the free
A timid silence in the home of the brave
With liberty and justice for those considered worthy
Who rose from the tyrannical arms of bigotry,
Who were taken as slaves,
They face hatred and violence
In America,
Land of the free,
Home of the brave
As we yell in anguish,
Our flag bloodied with murder,
Those we weren't able to save,
But a whisper is heard by our leaders
In America,
Land of the free,
Home of the brave
As a country,
A state of liberty and justice for all,
We must stop this eternal cycle of war and brawl,
In our thoughts we must engrave,
The victims and their names
In America,
Land of the free,
Home of the brave
Among the tragedy,
May we sing the melody of hope,
May we eternalize the objectives of those who precede us,
When confined in a period of grief,
We must look to the hope that once freed us
May we not fall in defeat,
But rather observe the foundation we have built under our feet,
An indubitable epiphany,
Absent of conflict and fight,
We must change as a nation,
As Americans we unite.
May we move forward,

Forgive our mistakes,
And restore beauty
In America,
Land of the Free,
Home of the Brave

AUDREY NEGRETE

Seeds to be Sown

Coming from fields baked by the sun
Where melons and grapevines grow
From brown hands picking from dusk til dawn
Even when no breezes blow

The pickers who came for a better life
Risking it all in their search
For a job and a home on different soil
Though not seen as of much worth

Though looked down upon they pick and box
The fruits to be taken and delivered
To someone far away from the Central Valley
Across streams and fields and rivers

So a fruit bowl is filled for a man as he awakens
And gets up to start the new day
Walking the streets, he passes his friend
She's going into the church to pray

In front of a shop sits an old, big-eyed dog
Whose owner is playing a guitar
The notes ringing out, set free by her fingers
To be heard by those near and far

But no music sings in the heart of the man
As he walks home from work that evening
One of his coworkers has been harassed
For his beliefs, and now he is leaving

Injustice burns through the blood of the man
At the casual company attitude
He believes people should be free to practice
Whatever faith or way of life they choose

He's tired of seeing people down on others
For the differences of which they're afraid
Each unkind word as though people aren't
All made of the same earth, different shades

The man gets home and immediately starts
To look for his suitcase and bags
When the telephone rings he answers it
And hears the voice of his dad

Son, I heard what happened there
And you feel you can't stay anymore
But I want you to take a moment and listen
Before you leave that seashore

Your mother and I came in search of a land
That would grant us the freedom to be
People who can make their own choices
People who can be free

But freedom comes with both joy and pain
For we take it into our own hands
And some people choose to do terrible things
And carry out terrible plans.

Son, I know that you want to leave
But your purpose isn't done
For you, too, have hands to make your choices
And you're meant to do good, my son.

Son, it's so wrong, what messed up things
Happen and take place every day
But son, when you're ready, you have a voice
And in America it has a say

From MLK Jr. speaking up and out
For he knew what had to be done
From women all over fighting for their rights
And who won't take 'no' from anyone

From the people who march out in our streets
Who demand the justice of change
All the songs of our land joining together
Demanding we say the names

From the artist standing back from their mural
To see their artwork alive

A message that will stay for many years
And be seen by many eyes

From the people who are not as this land promises
For their people who've never been free
From those who have fought and fight many battles
So that they might one day be

Everyone has a story like the changing day
We all share some shadow or light
We've all had joy in some shape or form
And all have our pain and fights

We have roots to anchor in this soil
So that our country can bloom
With the dreams and stories we hope it to hold
To overpower the broken gloom

That we can stand up and raise our voices high
Is a gift this country gives
For those whose lives are still going on
And for those who should have lived

Son, I know it's hard to see
The good in this country sometimes
But when we see the all the wrong and the bad
We can choose how it will be defined

By acceptance and heads facing toward the ground
Or blazing eyes and heads held high
Speak for the children of yesterday and tomorrow
For who we are and can be, in time.

Son, there is good coming down the road
That we have a chance to help pave
And amidst the thorns there are beautiful trees
The stories of the bold and the brave

The people who fought to make life better
For those who live in our land
The people who see the good that can come
When we look ahead and join hands

Look at all the seeds that we can sow
Like those who have lived here before us
There is hope for change and a better future
So let's join their mission and chorus.

The son looks down at the table beside him
A world of words in a dictionary
He says, "Okay dad, I'll think about it."
And flips to the word 'visionary'

Then he takes out a pen and a paper to write
What comes next, he doesn't quite know
But he unpacks his suitcase and all of his bags
For there are new seeds to be sown.

ANNEKA O'BRIEN

Stay United

As a new year starts and we start to transition
We see politicians competing for the position.

There are two sides, greatly divided
Each striding to hide the lies that each had provided.
We shall see how this new administration handles America,
It may lead to much despair...
Things may need to be repaired.

Many funds may be spent,
Most may not be meant.
Proven after 40 years to make no progress
America seems to be on a road to digress.

We should really be more united,
Instead, hatred is ignited.
We wonder where this path will lead
Because the nation has not agreed.

How is it justified to burn down buildings and break down statues?
It clearly does not show good virtues.

We shall hope for America that this does not continue,
And that we can all contribute
To the repairing of this nation.
While we live in isolation.

I hope this is a good change for our country
But this change can't come abruptly.
After these four years
Hopefully the fog clears.

What will it take?
What changes will we have to make?
We will have to face the winds of change,
Like a bird trying to fly a far range.

It might be difficult, like trogging through the snow
It might be difficult to overcome the differences in the country

It might be difficult to get along.
But it is necessary to thrive,
If this country is going to survive.

SABINA ORTOLAN

Special Day

Today is a special day

For those who fought,
For the families who lost those they loved,
For those who won't stop fighting for the beliefs they cherish

Today is a happy day

For those who hold their breath as they watch, read, and listen
For those who are ready to migrate into the future with a hopeful
mindset
For those who see the possibility of power, passion, knowledge

Today is a memorable day

Full of ambition, optimism,
promise and confidence

Today highlights new beginnings
Today highlights the possibility of what we could become
Today we witnessed a good day
A historical day.
A special day.

OLIVIA PEREZ

All Eyes on Us

The anticipation, the stress, the terror.
All eyes on our country.
The country that spiraled out of control.
The country that lost its meaning.
The country that lost its drive.
The country that lost its unity.

Unity, something that our country worked so hard to achieve, now
    seems unachievable.
Everyone is watching the country tear to shreds.
The division in this country is what will tear it apart but the two
    different sides will never just figure it out.
This isn't just about the two parties anymore.
It's about whether our country has a future.
It's about whether people in our country can feel safe

Every person must take a stand for the fate of our country is right in
    our hands.
One wrong move and we knock down a building that can't be rebuilt.
We need to make the right choice or we will live in our guilt.

Anxiety rising in every human being.
The very lives of people are at stake.
Choose to be ignorant or not but one wrong move is all it will take.

The world is on the line.
The world is burning.
All eyes on us, but what will be returning?

Everyone watched the news for hours and hours.
My hands are as sweaty as they get on a sunny day.
I couldn't bear to wait any longer.
Neither could the world.
We needed an answer.

Days and days pass and still no word.
People taking breaks from their jobs just to check the hourly news.
It seemed like forever.

The hours, minutes, and seconds elongating.
Yet still no word.

A dash of hope arrives when the news comes around.
Everyone is dancing all through town.
A sigh of relief from everyone I know.
We are giving our country a chance to re-grow.

ANDREW PETERS

Looking Forward

—After Elizabeth Alexander

Each day we **Praise**
Each other for doing good work, creating a **Song,**
Knowing there's something better down the road. **For**
We should forget the past, but remember the lessons it taught us.
    Walking
Into something we cannot yet see. Moving **Forward**
Following the mightiest word love, **In**
Everlasting trust we wallow. **That**
We can trust in our people, to follow the right path, into the brilliant
    Light.

LUKE POLONCHEK

Inaugural Poem

When I look outside, I wish to see the birds smiling, and the wind
  blowing,
Just as the people smile, and the city life blows
And if that happens, I'll know my job is done,
Because our country is our people,
And our people are our country.
I believe, a president is like a mother bird,
Watching, loving, and protecting all the little birds of America.
And if our country is sick, I will not turn my back.
The people come first, so I will also help neighbors who will help us,
My greatest wish is that our country will become the greatest in all the
  land,
Without losing our heart to the battle and our brains to the bronze.
I wish us to be respected, loved, and feared. So that way we can be a
  powerful country.
I also wish to love all people in our country, because there is strength in
  numbers and numbers is strength.
Only through love can we prosper and hate drives us back.
This has happened in the past, but no more will we be divided by red
  and blue.
Those are the colors that keep us together, not tear a seam in our flag.
I will fix this hole, and bring peace to America.

CHARLOTTE RAGOZIN

The Sun Rises

First over the Atlantic
Up and over the Appalachians
Then over the never ending corn fields
Over the Rockies
Rises over the Sierras
And lights up America

Then everyone wakes up
And hopes for a good day
But we all know
Some days are just hard
Especially some this past year

Maybe you are struggling with your mental health
Struggling to pay your rent
Struggling to get food on your plate
Or maybe you just do not want to get out of bed
These feelings are valid
Everyone feels this at some point

But, we are here today to celebrate a good day
To celebrate what is to come
A new president and vice president
A new vaccine for Covid-19
A new year full of opportunities

There is hope
There are better days to come
There are brighter days to come

EMILY RENTEL

Take Me Out to the Capital

Take me out to the capital
Fill the streets
with screams
Buy me some signs
and American flags
I'm here to
Stand for what's right

Let me root, root, root
for Biden
I'm now proud to
be an American
You got too many strikes
now you're finally out
Biden will make America great

MYLES RIPPBERGER

Work

Clean and tidy
Organized and proud
They stand happy and excited for another day
The classrooms filled with joy and excitement
The kids ignorant of the hard work
The parents frustrated at the workload
When will there be a break?
You look and see all the energy coming from the teachers
How?
Everyday they come ready for school
Each week the hours getting longer
Each grasp of comfort ripped away
When will it be over?
Procrastination isn't just a childish thing
The work so scary no one wants to touch it
Who will see the hours put in
Not the parents
Everyone so ignorant to the extra time
Why?
Why can't everyone see the time
You can say it's an easy job
Is it though?
The constant patience and energy needed
And for what?
What do they get out of it?
The underfunding
The low pay
How do they do it day in and day out
Why do it at all?
Quite a good question
One of many answers

AUDREY ROCK

As a Country

As a country we claim to be indivisible.
As a country we claim we live lives.
As a country we claim that people like you and I are resting with liberty
by our sides.
As a country we preach, as if justice is a gift handed to all.
But sooner than later, I can feel it coming in, at the rate of a wrecking
ball.
A voice that is deep within us will soon tell me that as a nation, we are
just this close to taking a fall.

People like me claim they know what it's like, to have to fight, and to
climb, a constant uphill hike.
An uphill hike we call freedom, that's so given to all.
We profess this concept as a nation, within these American walls.
Despite all of that, I see through a society that is toppling over; just
nearly about to fall.

We let appearance define us, until it's fully sunken within.
Some, but not all say, if your skin is not like the rest of us, your voice
must be a sin.
In a world still containing segregation, where small baby steps forward
are needed, can we please make a change; so many of us have
pleaded.
Our small section of the globe, known as the home of the brave, feels
overwhelmed with riots followed by suffering as well as injustice,
and our walls are beginning to cave.

Like a young one just beginning to crawl, we need stability and patience
to limit our falls.
If we don't work together, our civil section could soon go up in flames,
leaving future ancestors with this crazy structure of our country,
and the remembrance of our names.
We have rules and expectations written, are they too much to ask?
I'm only asking this question because so many citizens treat it as such a
huge task.
As a country we claim to be indivisible.
As a country we claim to live lives.
As a country we claim that people like you and I are resting with liberty
by our sides.

As a country we preach as if justice is a gift handed to all.
So everyone, please live up to the standards, before our nation fully
   comes to a crumble, and finally falls.

DANTE ROGERS

Follow the Rules

We have all seen it
The reign of Covid-19
It has lasted so long
March until past Halloween

For a year stuck indoors
While we all seek to find
Something to save us
Keep our families alive

The people who guide us
And are actually smart
Tell us it's simple
We all play a part

Some will refuse it
But all that they ask
To save your own life
Is to put on a mask

We still need to be careful
Yet now we can cope
A vaccine is coming
And with it new hope

Our leaders are changing
And so can we all
Follow the guidelines
Let the case count fall

We can beat it together
If we all stand as one
Stay at home now
For years later have fun

ITZEL SANCHEZ

Untitled

He must persevere
is this what it has come to
He is the **only** one who can help
The oldest at only **sixteen**
He might not see them for **years**
His **old** parents are struggling
But he is proud
he uses them as motivation
He **knows** they are depending on him
that this is how he will repay them
So he **does** what he must
The people here do **not** like him
But family **matter**s more
They want him to leave
If **only** they knew
They **See** a criminal
This will be **a** way to make his father proud
They know nothing of this **"intruder"**
Not a rapist, drug dealer, nor thug
a way to make mom less worried
The **caretaker** of the family
The **provider** for his sick father
Work **or** work were his options
The decision was not **hard**
Destined to be just another worker
So he steps up to the plate
he knows exactly what he was signed up for
But **keeps** his family in his heart
running from the dogs
Afraid of the voices yelling right behind him
to him it is a way out
He **look**s towards a better life for his future family
Send money **back** for them is the only mentality

KAIULANI SANCHEZ

What is This Virus?

What is this virus
It makes you really sick
Like is it the flu
Is it like a fish that is ich

They call it corona
I thought that was a beer
What is this virus
It is causing a lot of fear

What is this virus
That is so very severe
It's been keeping us in our house
For almost a whole year

When the country shut down
Our old lives did too
You weren't the only one
That was feeling so blue

Shutting the country down
Was a very bad move
All it did was destroy businesses
Because our numbers still improved

What is this virus
We now have a vaccine
Can we get back to normal
I'm tired of looking at a screen

RAYMI SHARP

We are Worth the Trouble

From 1776 we have been worth the trouble.
We have come together and been ripped apart.
We lean on one another seeking help.
For we all keep on walking.
Trying to understand the world.
Some are labeled better than others because of their beliefs.
Some are labeled more important because of their gender.
Some are talked down on, thought of as less worthy, all because of the
    simplicity of their skin.
But do we not all bleed the same blood and breathe the same brisk air?
Do we not all live on the same beautiful breathing Earth?
Not knowing where to go, only knowing to put one foot in front of
    the other?
Do we not all desire to live as one? In a world of peace?
Where the grass is lush, tall, tickled by a breeze.
We have come so far, yet we have so far to go.
Everyday taking another step, on a tricky path, toward a perfect world.
All together, him, her, you, and me.
We are all worth the trouble.
Don't you see?

SOPHIE SLUSHER

To the Betterment of Our Nation

—After Elizabeth Alexander

We **praise**
our progress, while the downtrodden sing the **song**
of sorrow, we stifle their cries **for**
the sake of patriotism, time is **walking**
onwards as our country stagnates and sours, the path **forward**
is led by our most neglected, we can find purpose **in**
the betterment of our broken nation, let us follow **that**
hopeful glimmer of **light**

HAILEE SMALLEY

Vibrant Petals

The Moon is just a big pile of rocks
And flowers are just weeds
But even with these descriptions
We only see the beauty and light
How the petals of a flower are bright and vibrant
How their smells bring the butterflies and bees

So why can't we just see the beauty in ourselves
Yes we are just big balls of flesh stomping on all the flowers
And hiding from the moon's glow,
But do you ever stop to consider how parts of our bodies were made
    to be touched?
Not in a strange way but in a way that makes us laugh and smile,
Or whenever we make a promise we lock pinkies to seal it?
We tend to forget these little things when we are feeling lost and blue,
So when you feel this way come back to this poem and say

"The moon is just a big pile of rocks"

STEPHANIE SPENCER

The Light of Change

On this day, we are still
Like a tree, with no wind to flow through its branches
Americans sit at home
Pondering on what life may have been
If things hadn't changed
We stare out our windows
Gazing at the sunset sky
Streaks of pink fluffy clouds
Remind us of cotton candy at carnivals
Oh, how we miss it
Remember carnivals?
Students, teachers
Mothers, fathers
Doctors, nurses
Mourning the loss of a different reality
A door that was closed
And shall never open again
Forced to enter a new door
Full of unknown
Remembering how just a year ago,
In this same country which we are now so unaccustomed to,
Teenagers encountered the issue of butterflies, fluttering around within
    them
When they saw that special someone
Schools were filled with laughter and life
Homes flooded with love and family
To every corner of every room
Today, living in a world
Full of deprivation
Feeling the sting of the wound that is cut so deep in our souls
So deeply wishing
Hoping
Begging
For the way life used to be
Walking at a distance
From those we long to be nearest
The urge to reach out
To be able to touch again
So strong that it moves you to tears

The feeling of your heart
Beating so loudly in your chest it's as loud as a thousand bass drums
You feel it start to break
As if someone took a hammer to a sheet of glass
And it shatters as you watch that dear friend continue on
Because you know that to come close would mean infection
Things have changed
There will always be change
Change is a constant
People change, the world will change
Everything can change
Whether for the better or the worse
Our future will be forever changed
We are growing
We are learning
We are one
The United States of America
As the sky shifts from light to dark
Flowers reach up towards the sky with awaiting arms
Waves crash on the shore and winds move mountains to their feet
As we persevere
Continue growing our minds
Encouraging each other to keep fighting
We'll take a leap
We'll forge ahead
All the change we have endured thus far
Will be worth the new change to come
Ideas swirl around in hurricanes
Until we reach the eye of the storm
All is calm for a moment
And we see that in the midst of it all,
We are surrounded by people
Right alongside us
A chain connected by each individual link
Marching through these changes in triumph
Just as we always do
After the storm there is light
A light so bright and warm it can melt the coldest of hearts
Our light is coming
The changes we endure
The losses we take
Will all be worth
The light of a new change for our United country

JASMINE STANDEZ

Untitled

The shared sun rises over expansive grasslands,
sparkling, snowy mountains
peering through shuttered windows,
spilling gold on the faces of America.

Bleary eyes look upon our country, the revered place of freedom
hoping this will be their day,
this their moment.

Sleep shaken away, uniforms donned, truckers snake their silver trucks
     cross-country,
Teachers slide on glasses, the future of America waiting in their
     classrooms,
Farmers pluck strawberries, straw hats palm trees over a desert of
     crops.

Some bleakly stare at a hazy skyline,
hoping for time to make a change.
As the ozone layer chokes on pollution.

Dread fills the hearts of those pleading for a future,
as unexpected fires ravage hope, floating away with plastics discarded
     into the sea.

The scars of the past poison today,
remnants strangling those who have fought so hard.
Dripping blood and sweat
for the promise of America
only received with its beauty stained by the cynicism required to
     survive.

And yet.
We still hope.
Hope for change.
Hope for true equality.
Hope for a future slowly, slipping away.

Hope not lost,
only scattered seeds in a field of stone.

But alive.
Seeking the kiss of elements, a blessing to stretch out roots, a crack in
    the steely facade.

Shadows of pain leech compassion, spark selfishness.
I take what I need to make it.
Worn hearts of America close,
drowning the budding tendrils of selflessness in cold velvet.

Our roots intertwine but
our sunflower faces look to different stars.

And yet.

We long,
For our cold-glass country to warm.
For unity, connection.
To release the spark tightly closed in our fist,

Each person a radiating accomplishment
in this lovely land.

For a moment, we all look towards our shared sunrise,
our sparks blazing.
We all fight for everyone and ourselves
Full of love.

The caged wings of America stretch, shine down promise, iridescent in
    every sparkling eye.

CORALYNE TAYLOR

Rivers of Words

Rivers of words
Flowing from the roots
The rice, the cacao, the wheat, the corn, and the yucca.
Their roots form roads on a map
Making their way through the soil
Intertwining to create a tomorrow
A tomorrow worth watering.

JOEY VETRONE

United or Divided

The United States of America
Unity
The state of being united
Joined as a whole

Does this accurately represent America
Citizens beginning to focus
Solely on their own success
Caused a loss of unity for the rest

War after war
Battle after battle
We've grown farther apart
And need to come back together

As people begin to identify themselves
And respect themselves
Instead of worrying about ourselves
We hated and criticized someone else

Currently divided
The goal is to unite us
For we need a break
To show love instead of hate

For too many lives have been taken
From nothing more than opinion
We need to stand together with 6ft of distance
To become one and prove our existence

The road to recovery
Lies at our feet
And to sit back and watch
Is to accept our defeat

Our defeat as a whole
Our defeat as one
So let's come together
And I'll show you what we can become.

MIA VILLALOBOS

This Last Year

This year, the invisible year
The year of the unexpected
With up and downs
Yet there is no direction
Stay 6 ft away or be infected
Use hand sanitizer to disinfect it
A virus that is contagious
But the President neglects it

Then all of the sudden
Virus doesn't matter
All we can hear
Is black lives matter
George Floyd, an innocent man
Father figure, son of the light
Accused with no right
An uncommitted crime
He is pinned to the ground
Resistance is felt
Resilience is deep
Resting may he be

Painfully hurting
Our nation is suffering
Yet somehow with hope
We learn to cope
Unclear of the future
We must decide
Is it blue? Is it red?
Is it left? Is it right?
Is what is best
For our children's lives

The hearts of our nation
Are filled with desire
Strength must prevail
Love must survive
Hope is the force
That drives our desire

Together in one
We will fight for our rights

SAM WEATHERLY

America

America, a nation of the free and home of the brave,
It changes like a growing willow and works like a rushing river.
The city light flashing like fireflies in the night, and people bustling like
    bees in the day.
The choice to believe what you wish and do as you please.
Growing up here has its highs and its lows, but it will always be my
    home.
This is what America is to me.
From the swamplands in the south to the plains in the west
From the cold in the north, to the warm in the south
There is no other nation I would rather call my own
This is what America is to me.

ABIGALE WEE

Growing Home

There's a certain endearment
About the black and white tiles on the floor
of Toy Boat Dessert Cafe,
the lingering smell of coffee,
the figurines that line the wall.
I grew a piece of home
in the table next to
the ice-cream-sticky rocking horse.

I planted a seed of home
between the rocks leading
to the creek where time
seems to flow like honey
and the leaves above make verdant
stained glass. I watered it
with trust and peace
so I would never forget
the home I found in friendship.

There's the sprout of home among the faded blue seats
that stand as silent sentinels
in the 3:42 Southbound Caltrain
from Hillsdale station.
In the Debussy that plays
to the sound of the train, the people
who seem to live
in a world of their own.

In the place where the waves crash
like cymbals against the grainy sand
revealing shards of shells
and frosty sea glass,
I hid a tendril of home inside the wave-battered wood.
I watched as it sent roots, giving life
to the tired grey trunk of the fallen tree.

The ecstasy of performance is woven
into every branch of my home, like amber
strung on gold wire.

Amber for the last note of the piece,
the sweet exhaustion as I relinquish
my hold on the burning energy
that fills my veins when I play music for others.

When I step back
and look up, towards the sun,
I see the leaves and branches of an oak tree.
My feet stand next to gnarled roots
that stem from the little seeds of home
that I scattered
and tended around the bay.

And I know
the oak-tree-home I nurtured
mapped by the roots on the ground
will continue to grow.

EMETT WHITE

The Land of the Free

And the home of the brave
I think of this saying
each and every day

From Plymouth Rock
to the golden gate bridge
Our country stands tall
and our people unbound

Depending not on experience
nor on appearance
if you live in this country
Then you are free

You are free to speak out
you are free to worship
you are free to be
whoever you want

The land of the free
And the home of the brave
I think of this saying
each and every day

STEPHAN WIEGOLD

A Distant Thing

Hope is a distant thing.

It is not seen, smelled, tasted, felt, or heard.
It only remains as a visage, a chased phantom.

The only evidence of its existence stays as imprints of what once was,

The freshly wetted streets of the morning,
The orange sky with no sun,
The half-sunken deer bones.

The bystanders only look on with hollow eyes, in the shadow.

Hope is a distant thing.

Found only by those willing to stalk its tracks, and crawl through the
thick stinging nettle.
Though, the determined hunter is not left unrewarded.

At the end of the beast-prints they find their treasure,

The sacred midnight storm,
The painted sky and glorious sun of dusk,
The holy feast of the mountain lion.

The hunters only look on with hopeful eyes, in the distant.

KAI ZANETTE

We Wish We Were Kids Again

Happy and giddy we ran around
As little kids.
Now we sit at home
Buried in our cell phones, televisions, and computers.
Oh the cold winter we are in
We must stay inside and flip through the channels
Only to find Elf for the twelfth time today.

Now we must stay at home or wear protection
No friends and no parties allowed anymore.
Just a simple stay at home order.
No joy and no happiness we get from seeing other people anymore
No more class clown or your crush just down the hall.
It has all vanished like a bat in the night sky.

Oh what we'd do to run around and play again
On the jungle gyms and the play structures
To make good ol' memories like Papa Joe said.

Now we stare out our windows wondering what it would be like to
    have it all back.
As we can only hope it gets better day in and day out
As we watch life go 'round and 'round
We think of the days we were happy and giddy where we ran around.

PORTOLA VALLEY FIRST GRADERS

Woodland Poem

You can put anything
on the magic paper

Shining sun
Pollen for bugs

Flying in the water
Eating fish

Cold yummy
Ice cream

I love watermelons
On a hot summer day

Sunny days
Play catch

Skraps like little
Vagume cleeners

Peeps are yummy
Nature is awesome

The beautiful white petals
Are like unicorn mane

The keys on the piano
Are sparkling like bubbly water

I see a sparkling sunset
With the colors green and purple

Rain falls
The deer look for shelter

She looks like a wild fox
She runs like no one's there

This leaf is ripped
Like a broken wing

Can you love, love?
Yes, everyone can love, love.

Some are easy
Some are hard

Family is all healthy
Heart is full like a cheerful bird

When my mom is not around
I feel very lonely

My dog
Needs lots of love

My dog
Likes to eat my food

I see myself
There's a copy of me

It looks
Like white and pink cotton candy

It looks like
A sunset could be a tree

ACKNOWLEDGMENTS

Deepest gratitude to the following educators and advocates for fostering an appreciation for poetry and community-building in San Mateo County's youth and for organizing and/or supporting poetry-related projects in 2020:

San Mateo County Board of Supervisors
San Mateo County Arts Commission
San Mateo County Housing Leadership Council (HLCSMC)
San Mateo County Libraries
Peninsula Library System
Ms. Monica Gojcaj, Teacher at Woodland School
Ms. Ivana Hansen, Teacher at Woodland School
Ms. Victoria Maier Magbilang, Executive Director of the Daly City Public Library Associates and Founder, Daly City Youth Poet Laureate Program
Ms. Robin Rodricks, Director Emerita of the San Mateo County Arts Commission
Ms. Leora Tanjuatco Ross, Associate Director of the Housing Leadership Council of San Mateo County and Co-organizer of the 2020 San Mateo County Youth Poetry & Arts Competition
Mr. Jim Ward, Teacher and Fall Play & Spring Musical Director at Half Moon Bay High School

Many thanks especially to our young people who, while distance learning, remained engaged and found ways to connect with their communities, participating in poetry workshops, classes and contests throughout the year. They are the best of us.

ABOUT THE CONTRIBUTORS

Denely Acosta, a sophomore in high school, loves to play soccer, play with her brother and usually video games.

Evan Alexander is a sophomore in high school. He enjoys playing tennis and video games, and also plays the saxophone for the high school band.

Luke Aranda is a sophomore in high school and plays basketball for his school team.

Noel Atkinson is a sophomore in high school and is currently not being able to do sports, but loves football and hanging out with friends.

Grace Bigelow-Leth is a sophomore in high school and loves to play beach volleyball, indoor volleyball, golf, and go to the beach.

Conner Black is a sophomore in high school who enjoys playing beach volleyball, running, sketching, hanging out with her friends.

Brian Booher is a sophomore in high school and plays tennis and water polo.

Maya Boysen is a sophomore in high school. She enjoys playing soccer.

Camryn Bye is a sophomore in high school and plays softball for the school. She enjoys skiing in her free time.

Eleanor Carpenter (Nori) is a sophomore in high school who plays beach volleyball and indoor volleyball. She loves music and shopping.

Devon Chaney is a sophomore in high school. He enjoys swimming and spending time with his family

Abigaile "Abby" Co is a sophomore in high school and enjoys playing basketball.

Allison Co is a sophomore in high school. She enjoys playing basketball, golf, waterpolo, and walking her dog.

Trevor Coruccini is a sophomore who plays basketball and baseball, and enjoys his math class.

Ronit Das is a fifth grader and a finalist in the HLCSMC Youth Poetry & Arts Competition.

Bela Davila is a sophomore in high school. She loves fashion, enjoys singing, and plays tennis for the team at her high school.

Hannah De Leon is a sophomore in high school and enjoys hanging out with friends, going on adventures, and exploring the outdoors.

Alli Dioli is a sophomore in high school who loves playing basketball, walking her dogs, and spending time with family and friends.

Drew Dorwin is a sophomore who loves to play basketball and hang with friends.

Coco Dubose is a sophomore in high school. She likes going to the beach, hanging out with her friends and playing with her dog.

Cole Eckert is a sophomore in high school who enjoys going biking, skiing, as well as playing soccer.

Mia Etheridge is a sophomore in high school. She loves to play volleyball and go to the beach with her friends.

Nora Flynn is a sophomore. She enjoys volunteering at a local farm and cooking in her spare time.

Lily Fortin is a sophomore in high school.

Jordan Girard is a sophomore in high school. She likes to play volleyball and go to the beach.

Elijah Gjovig is a sophomore in high school.

Kaia Glafkides is a sophomore in high school. She loves spending time with family and friends. Her favorite subjects in school are History and English.

Scarlett Glazebrook is a sophomore in high school. She plays tennis and swims. She also enjoys traveling, hanging out with friends, and sleeping.

Alexa Godoy is a sophomore in high school. She enjoys going to the beach and spending time with family and friends.

Jacob Goldstein is a sophomore in high school. He plays water polo for the school and enjoys skateboarding and surfing.

Valeria Lopez Gonzalez is a sophomore in high school. She enjoys hanging out with friends.

Iris Grant is a sophomore in high school and a competitive athlete, playing both volleyball and basketball.

Kaylani Guevara is a sophomore in high school. She loves playing soccer and waterpolo, and seeing her friends.

Kaiya Hanepen is a sophomore in high school. She plays water polo, surfs, and snowboards.

Liam Harrington and **Ryan Harrington** are sophomores in high school. They are twins.

Hailey Hernandez is a sophomore in high school. She plays volleyball and softball. She loves to travel places with her family and loves to hangout with her friends.

Kay Hildebrand is a sophomore in high school. She plays water polo and basketball, and surfs.

Callie Hoffman is a sophomore in high school and plays soccer and water polo for the school.

AnaSofia Infanzon-Marin is a high school sophomore and a competitive ice skater. She has been doing musical theatre since the 6th grade and she likes plants.

Jade Ireland is a sophomore in high school. They adore riding horses, acting in plays, and being with friends.

Emily Jenar plays volleyball for the high school and also plays club indoor and beach volleyball. She loves going to the beach and taking her dog for walks.

Julian Jimenez is a sophomore in high school. He plays American football and soccer. He also enjoys running and playing video games.

Ana Johnston is a sophomore in high school. She enjoys volunteering at SPCA, traveling around the world, and spending time with her friends.

Dominic Katout is a sophomore in high school. He dreams of being a game designer and in his opinion, to understand game design, one must see how other forms of art allow you to experience and feel certain things.

Josephine "Josie" Kearns is a sophomore in high school. She is also a competitive gymnast. She has two sisters and a dog.

Alex Koron is a sophomore in high school. He enjoys taking his dog to the beach.

Kaija Laakes is not a part of any school clubs or sports, but she sings and has been roller skating all of her life.

Ashley Lau is a sophomore in high school and a finalist in the HLCSMC Youth Poetry & Arts Competition.

Kai Lester is a sophomore in high school. He enjoys playing volleyball and cheerleading.

Kai Fujino Lin is a sophomore in high school. He likes playing tennis as an extracurricular activity, and loves to write poems in his free time.

Jescent Marcelino, a sophomore in high school, recently immigrated from the Philippines.

Sadhbh McClenaghan is a sophomore in high school. She enjoys playing volleyball and soccer.

Sydney McGuirk is a sophomore in high school. She enjoys swimming, surfing, water polo, along with anything to do with the water.

Madison Melo is a sophomore in high school. She loves the beach and exploring the outdoors.

Makala Mesina-Forester is a sophomore in high school. She is on the cheer team and is in the school musicals. Makala enjoys playing the piano and hanging out with her friends.

Moss Michelsen is a sophomore in high school.

Owen Miller is a sophomore in high school and enjoys sports.

Riley Mills is a sophomore in high school and enjoys playing volleyball and painting.

Alessandra Morales is a sophomore in high school. She enjoys wrestling and playing water polo.

Belinda Morales is a sophomore in high school. She enjoys painting and hanging out with her friends.

Elle Morris is a sophomore in high school. She enjoys volleyball and being with her friends.

Madi Mullins, a sophomore in high school, enjoys playing volleyball, painting, and playing the piano.

Sofia Nadeau is a sophomore in high school. She enjoys playing the piano, traveling, and baking.

Akhilendra Nair is in his sophomore year. He enjoys playing basketball and enjoying free time with friends.

Audrey Negrete is a sophomore in high school and enjoys writing, playing the harp, animals, and doing Brazilian jiu jitsu.

Anneka O'Brien is a sophomore in high school. She enjoys playing softball and spending time with animals. She also enjoys hanging out with friends.

Sabina Ortolan is a sophomore in high school. She enjoys playing soccer and going to the beach. She also enjoys time with friends and family.

Olivia Perez is a sophomore in high school.

Andrew Peters is a 16 year old who plays soccer for the high school. He enjoys skiing, mountain biking, and surfing.

Luke Polonchek is 15 years old. He is on the surf team and has a twin brother and a little sister.

Portola Valley First Graders wrote every line in their collaborative poem, accompanied with drawings. Each student contributed a couplet.

Charlotte Ragozin is a sophomore in high school. She enjoys playing tennis, traveling to new places, and spending time with friends.

Emily Rentel is a sophomore in high school. She plays softball and loves listening to music and spending time with friends.

Myles Rippberger is a sophomore in high school.

Audrey Rock, a 10th grader, plays tennis, loves running on the beach, and enjoys spending time with family and friends.

Dante Rogers is a high school sophomore. He likes to spend time outdoors and read books.

Itzel Sanchez is a sophomore in high school. She enjoys spending time with her dog and family.

Kaiulani Sanchez is a sophomore in high school. She enjoys playing soccer and spending time at the beach.

Raymi Sharp is an enthusiastic learning student who loves the beach!

Sophie Slusher is a sophomore in high school. She enjoys creating art, kickboxing, and collecting records.

Hailee Smalley is a sophomore in high school. She enjoys writing, horseback riding, and spending time with her family and friends.

Stephanie Spencer is a sophomore in high school. She plays tennis, basketball, runs track and loves to go to the beach.

Jasmine Standez plays volleyball and is a sophomore in high school. She loves to do art, sing, and read.

Coralyne Taylor is a sophomore in high school.

Joey Vetrone is a sophomore and spends her time playing indoor and beach volleyball yearlong. She enjoys hanging out with her friends, reading, and writing.

Mia Villalobos is a sophomore in high school. She plays soccer and loves to go to the beach and explore nature.

Sam Weatherly is a sophomore in high school. He enjoys spending time with his friends and ocean surfing.

Abigale Wee is a freshman in high school and first place winner of the countywide Housing Leadership Council Youth Poetry & Arts Competition.

Emett White is a sophomore in high school.

Stephan Wiegold loves trees and mountains and is a sophomore in high school.

Kai Zanette is a sophomore, plays football and baseball, and likes to hang out with friends.

Made in the USA
Las Vegas, NV
23 June 2021